in tokyo this would be a palace

edition axel menges

martin rendel, rené spitz (eds.)   das weite suchen *expanding the gap*

das weite suchen *expanding the gap* / hg. von martin rendel, rené spitz
© 2002 edition axel menges, stuttgart / london
isbn 3-932565-28-2

alle rechte vorbehalten, besonders die der übersetzung in andere sprachen.
all rights reserved, especially those of translation into other languages.

reproduktionen *reproductions*: l+n litho, waiblingen
druck *printing*: druckhaus münster, kornwestheim

übersetzung *translation into english*: lunn drabble gmbh, essen
entwurf *design*: rendel & spitz gmbh, köln
schrift *typeface*: frutiger condensed, transit italic
papier *paper*: römerturm agento

architekten des gebäudes *architects of the building*: b&k+, köln

inhalt *content*

das projekt *the project*   6

die gäste *the guests*
ross lovegrove   16
greg lynn   28
tokujin yoshioka   42

weitere beiträge *further contributions*
köbi gantenbein   54
hannes heer   74

die vorbereitungen *the preparations*   90
das ergebnis *the result*   104

das projekt *the project*

wie kommt das neue in die welt?

    aufrecht und gelassen. Durch den haupteingang. Unaufgefordert. Konstantin grcic hatte sich mit dem neuen verabredet. Am abend des 17. januar, gegen 22 uhr, gesellte sich ross lovegrove zu unserer feier des passagenprojekts «mut zur lücke». Als wir ihn begrüßten, sah er sich um und strahlte: «in tokyo this would be a palace». Ein seltsamer, ein schöner gedanke.

    wir wußten noch nicht, daß wir ross lovegrove im laufe des abends spontan dazu einladen sollten, das ausstellungsprojekt für die nächsten «passagen» anzuführen – in der rolle, die zuvor konstantin grcic übernommen hatte. Wir wußten noch nicht einmal, ob wir 2002 überhaupt wieder ein ausstellungsprojekt mit drei designern aus aller welt initiieren wollten. Wir wußten nur, daß wir sehr müde von den anstrengungen der vorangegangenen tage waren.

how does the new come into the world?

    upright and calmly. Through the main entrance. Unasked. Konstantin grcic had a date with the new. On the evening of 17 january, at about 10 p.m., ross lovegrove joined our celebration of the passagen project «daring the gap». When we greeted him he looked around and smiled: «in tokyo, this would be a palace». A strange, a beautiful thought.

    we did not yet know that we would spontaneously invite ross lovegrove over the course of the evening to lead the exhibition project for the next «passagen» – in the role that konstantin grcic had previously taken over. We did not know whether or not we even wanted to initiate another exhibition project with three designers from around the world in 2002. We only knew that we were extremely tired after the efforts of the preceding days.

die permanente anspannung löste sich gerade. In den ersten tagen hatten erstaunlich viele besucher den geforderten «mut zur lücke» bewiesen. Besonders das interesse der internationalen presse überraschte uns, schließlich nahmen wir zum ersten mal an den «passagen» teil. Das fachpublikum und die journalisten ließen sich von der eigenwilligen atmosphäre bezaubern, die durch das zusammenspiel von architektur, farbigem licht, riesigem gummiball, duftinstallationen und behaglicher wärme an der feuerstelle entstanden war. Um ein abgedroschenes wort zu bemühen: es war ein erlebnis. Eines, dessen wirkung wir zuerst kaum angemessen einschätzten, weil wir zu sehr mit seiner ermöglichung beschäftigt waren.

the constant stress had just begun to subside. During the first days an amazing number of visitors had demonstrated the required «daring the gap». We were especially surprised by the interest shown by the international press – after all, this was the first time that we had participated in the «passagen». The professional audience and journalists became enchanted with the very individual atmosphere that was created through the interaction of architecture, colored light, a huge rubber ball, scent installations and a comfortable warmth at the fireplace. To employ a much-used phrase: it was an experience. An experience whose effect we at first could hardly assess properly because we were much too busy making it all possible.

dieser zauber läßt sich am besten damit beschreiben, daß viele, viele besucher mit einem freundlichen und aufrichtigen «danke» die ausstellung verließen. Sie bedankten sich für ein geschenk, von dem wir anfangs nicht geahnt hatten, wie schön es würde.

und nun, zur feier, platzte der raum aus allen nähten. Die gäste kamen so schnell und so zahlreich, daß das bier noch nicht bereitstand – in köln eine unmöglichkeit, so als ob dem kardinal zum hochamt das weihwasser ausgegangen wäre. Das ehepaar gruber hatte wohl die gastronomische katastrophe vorausgesehen und zückte den vorsorglich mitgebrachten eigenen prosecco. Dann betrat ross lovegrove den raum.

«in tokyo this would be a palace» – seine erste assoziation erwies sich als leitfaden für das neue projekt. Als wir einige wochen später kontakt mit ross lovegrove aufnahmen, um unsere mündlich ausgesprochene einladung zu wiederholen, sprachen wir über die beiden kollegen, die er auswählen wollte. Sein erster blick richtete sich nach tokio: tokujin yoshioka sollte mit von der partie sein. Als dritten im bunde wünschte er sich greg lynn, andere himmelsrichtung.

die weite von ross lovegroves vorstellungskraft, die unsere kargen räume mit der pracht eines palastes assoziierte, knüpfte nun ein band zwischen designern aus drei kontinenten. Der knoten war in köln geschürzt. Das motto des neuen projektes «das weite suchen / expanding the gap» drückte aus, daß raum auszudehnen sei – während in «mut zur lücke / daring the gap» der schmale raum noch schmaler gemacht worden war.

this charm can be best described as follows: many, many visitors left the exhibition with a friendly and sincere «thank you». They thanked us for a gift, the beautiful outcome of which we were unaware in the beginning.

and now, at the celebration, the space was bursting at the seams. The guests came so quickly and numerously that the beer could not flow quickly enough – a ridiculous thought in cologne, like the cardinal running out of holy water during the missa solemnis. The gruber couple must have anticipated the gastronomic catastrophe and served the prosecco they had brought along to be on the safe side. And then ross lovegrove entered the room.

«in tokyo this would be a palace» – his first association was to become the guide for the new project. When we contacted him a few weeks later to repeat our invitation, we spoke about the two colleagues he wanted to choose. His first glance was directed towards tokyo: tokujin yoshioka was to be one, and he wanted greg lynn – other cardinal point – to be the third.

the breadth of ross lovegrove's imagination that associated our austere spaces with the splendor of a palace now tied a link between designers from three continents. The knot was pulled taut in cologne. The motto of the new project, «das weite suchen / expanding the gap», expressed the idea that space could be expanded – whereas the narrow space was made even narrower in «mut zur lücke / daring the gap.»

 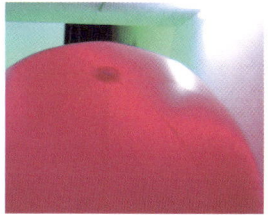  

«das weite suchen» war nicht nur das neue thema. Es illustrierte auch die umstände der vorbereitungen. Wenn wir am einen telefonhörer mit greg lynn und am anderen mit tokujin yoshioka telefonierten, befanden wir uns auf der insel des vorigen tages, denn es war gleichzeitig 6 uhr morgens, 12 uhr mittags und 20 uhr abends.

«das weite suchen» hat uns gelehrt, daß man auch bei engen grenzen, die von außen gesetzt sind, der beschränktheit entfliehen kann. Um das weite zu suchen, brauchen wir uns nicht zu entfernen. Wir brauchen die weite welt nur einzuladen. Dann besucht sie unsere nähe. Wir tun es gern auch im nächsten jahr.

rendel & spitz
köln, im januar 2002

«expanding the gap» was not only the new theme but it also illustrated the circumstances behind the preparations. When we spoke with greg lynn on one phone and with tokujin yoshioka on another it was simultaneously 6 a.m., 12 noon and 8 p.m.

«expanding the gap» has taught us that we can escape the confines even with narrow limits that are dictated from the outside. To expand the gap we don't have to remove ourselves. We only have to invite the world. Then it will visit our space. We will be happy to do it again next year.

rendel & spitz
cologne, january 2002

die gäste *the guests*

ross lovegrove

ross lovegrove, london

die vorstellung, wie der raum entweder durch physische oder virtuelle mittel manipuliert werden kann, ist meiner meinung nach das eigentlich wesentliche an der arbeit von uns dreien, die wir in diesem jahr eingeladen wurden, den begriff des projektes von rendel & spitz zu erweitern. Wir alle haben uns der leidenschaft verschrieben, materialien und prozesse zu erforschen, die uns zu aufregenden, neuen erfahrungen in unserer sich entwickelnden physischen welt führen.

the concept of exploring the way space can be manipulated either through physical or virtual means is i believe something intrinsic in the work of the three of us who have been invited this year to expand the perception of the rendel & spitz project. We all share a passionate level of enquiry into materials and processes that are leading us towards exciting new experiences in our evolving physical world.

dieses projekt reflektiert daher den gemeinsamen standpunkt dreier menschen, die in derselben welt mit derselben motivation und vorstellungskraft leben, trotz der großen physischen entfernung, die uns trennt.

this project therefore reflects common ground for three people living in the same world with the same motivation and spirit despite the great physical distances that separate us.

im atelier von
ross lovegrove
*in ross love-
grove's studio*

bei unserer ersten begegnung hier in london stellten wir ein gemeinsames interesse an der erweiterung des raums fest, entweder indem die äußere welt nach innen gekehrt oder indem die verborgene architektur durch das verwischen der grenzen verzerrt wird. Im rahmen dieser vorstellung habe ich nach wegen gesucht, meine eigenen persönlichen gedanken über die schaffung organischer dreidimensionaler oberflächen mit der am wenigsten invasiven installationsmethode, nämlich der digitalen projektion, zu kombinieren. Die besucher werden hoffentlich etwas erfahren, das kinetisch und ständiger verwandlung unterworfen ist, während sie gleichzeitig etwas passives und beruhigendes spüren; das verbindende element zwischen der spirituell sensitiven auffassung meines freundes tokujin und den visionären architektonischen dreidimensionalen formen meines freundes greg.

ich hoffe, eines tages noch einmal mit ihnen ausstellen zu können, und zwar unter dem titel: «übernatürlich».

our first encounter here in london revealed a shared interest in ways to expand the space either by bringing the outside world inside or by distorting the dormant architecture, through blurring the boundaries. Within this concept i have studied ways to link my own personal thoughts of how to create organic free form surfaces with the least invasive method of installation, that of digital projection. People who visit will hopefully experience something that is kinetic and ever changing whilst at the same time feel something passive and calming that is a linking statement somewhere between the spiritually sensitive understanding of my friend tokujin and the visionary architechtonic three dimensional forms of my friend greg.

one day i hope to exhibit with them once again under the title «supernatural».

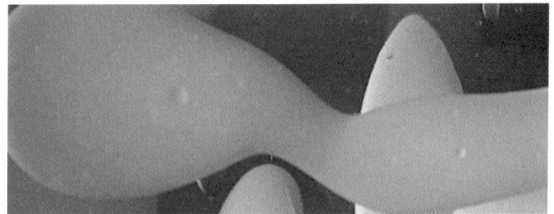

die gäste *the guests*

greg lynn

greg lynn, los angeles

«bibliographie» «*bibliography*»
animate form, book and interactive cd- rom (new york: princeton architectural press, 1999). Folds, bodies & blobs: collected essays, (bruxelles: encore books by architects, 1998). Any magazine, editorial board member, 1992-present. Lightness: any magazine no. 5, «differential gravities,» co-editor with john rajchman (new york: any co., 1993). Folding in architecture, ad special issue no.102, «architectural curvilinearity: folded, pliant & supple architecture» & «stranded sears tower,» editor with an introduction (london: academy additions, 1993). Fetish, co-editor and designer with e. mitchell & s. whiting, (new york: princeton architectural press, 1992). 2g: landscape architecture, (barcelona, 1997), pps. 34-39. 40 under 40, (vitae publishing, 1996). 5000 artists return to artists space: 25 years, «interview with claudia gould» (new york: artists space, 1998), 285. A+U, no. 321, «korean presbyterian church & h2 pavilion» (tokyo: a+u publishing co., ltd., june 1997), cover & 82-111. Any 0: writing in architecture, no.0, «probable geometries: writing architecture within the body» (new york: any co., 1993). Any magazine no. 7: colin rowe, «new variations: rowe complex,» (new york: any co., september, 1994). Any magazine, «charles gwathmey: a physique out of proportion» (new york: any co., 1995). Any magazine, no.14: tectonics unbound, «blobs (or why tectonics is square and topology is groovy)» (new york: any co., 1996). Any magazine, no. 23: diagram work, «embryological housing» (new york: any co., 1998). Anybody, «from body to blob» (new york, 1997), pps. 162-173. Anytime, «bio time» (new york: any co., 1999), 266-271. Anywise, «form and field» (new york, 1996), pps. 92-99. Arch+: die architektur des ereignisses, no. 119-120, «multiplicitous and in-organic bodies,» (berlin, december 1993). Arch+: die entfaltung der architektur, «probable geometries: writing architecture within the body» (berlin, 1993). Arch+: information: faltung in der architektur, «das gefaltete, das biegsame und das geschmeidige» (berlin, may 1996). Arch+: leicht und schwer, no.124-125, «differential gravities» & «cad-journal 21: special effects in architecture» (berlin, december 1994). Arch+: von berlin nach neuteutonia, no. 122, «von der komplexitat zur postmoderne?» (berlin, june 1994). Architectural design, no.107: organic architecture, «multiplicitous and in-organic bodies,» (london: academy additions, 1993), pps. 30-37. Architectural design, no.127: architecture after geometry, «an advanced from of movement,» (london: academy additions, 1997), pps. 54-57. Architectural profile, no. 2, vol. 1 (bangkok,

los angeles
aus der sicht von
franz schnaas
*los angeles seen by
franz schnaas*

1996), pps. 90-97. Architectural record, «the easier beauty of animate form: greg lynn's recent projects, the embryological house and the korean presbyterian church, challenge our assumptions about aesthetics,» by ann bergren (november 2000), 78-82. Architectural record, «embryologic house» (december 1999), 104-109. Architecture + urbanism, no. 276, «stranded sears tower» (tokyo: a+u publishing co., ltd., september 1993). Architecture + urbanism, no. 281, «the intensive disappearance of weil arets» (tokyo: a+u publishing co., ltd., february, 1994), pps. 138-143. Architecture + urbanism, no.321, «korean presbyterian church and omv exhibition pavilion» (tokyo: a+u publishing co., ltd., june 1997), pps. 82-111. Architecture magazine, «digital conversion» by j. giovannini (october, 1999), cover, 2 & 87-99. Architecture magazine, «virtual promise» by r. kroloff & «computer worship» by j. giovannini (october 1999), cover, 2-3 & 87-99. Architecture magazine, «virtual promise» by reed kroloff & «computer worship» by joseph giovannini (october 1999), cover, 2-3 & 87-99. Architecture magazine: 1997 awards issue, (new york: january 1997), pps. 80-81. Architecture magazine: 1997 awards issue, (new york: january 1997), 80-81. Architektur aktuell, «kohärenz im kosmos, order: diagramme in kostümen,» by b. lootsma, (june 2000)

122-133. Architexturally speaking: ten untenured faculty, «stranded sears tower» (chicago: gallery 400, 1992), 12-13. Arhitektov bilten, no.115/116, february 1993, «intenzivno izginevanje intensive disappearance» (ljubljana, 1993). Arquitectura 289, «the deference of anyone» (madrid: college of architecture at university of madrid, october 1991). Art in america, «design: sleeker, thinner, sexier» by s. cash, (june 2000) 50-53. Artbyte, «embryological house» interview with m. dery (november 2000). Assemblage 19, «multiplicitous and in-organic bodies» (cambridge, mass.: mit press, 1993). Assemblage 26, «the renewed novelty of symmetry: cardiff bay opera house competition project» (cambridge, mass.: mit press, 1995). Assemblage 26, «the renewed novelty of symmetry: cardiff bay opera house competition project» (cambridge, mass.: mit press, 1995). Assemblage 29, «in the wake of the avantgarde» (cambridge, mass.: mit press, 1996). Assemblage 38, «korean presbyterian church of new york, queens, new york city» (cambridge, mass.: mit press, 1999), 6-21. Assemblage 38, «mark rakatansky, subject: greg lynn» (cambridge, mass.: mit press, 1999), 22-28. Assemblage no. 38, «korean presbyterian church of new york, queens, new york city» (cambridge, mass.: mit press, 1999), 6-28. Bauwelt, review

lincoln boulevard

of animate form by christian brensing (no. 1, 2000), pp. 41. Berlage papers, «blobs» (amsterdam: berlage institute, 1996). Blueprint: architecture, design & contemporary culture, «re-made in america» by r. ryan (october, 1999: no. 165), 44-47. Blueprint: architecture, design & contemporary culture, «re-made in america» by raymund ryan (october, 1999: no. 165), 44-47. Cahier #6: witte de with (july 96), pps. 93-104. Cahiers, no. 6, «frederick kiesler, architect» (rotterdam: witte de with, july 1997). Cities on the move, (bourdeaux 1998). Cities on the move: urban chaos and global change, east asian art, architecture and film now, «embryological housing» (london: hayward gallery, 1999), 50. Columbia: the magazine of columbia university, «the new wave in architecture: columbia architects harness computer wizardry to lead revolutions in design and practice» by jill herbers (columbia, winter 1999) pps. 36-37. Cream: contemporary art in culture (10 curators, 10 writers, 100 artists), (bristol, uk: phaidon press, 1998). Cream: contemporary art in culture (10 curators, 10 writers, 100 artists), phaidon press (group show through publication), arnolfini, bristol, uk, 15 october 1998. Daidalos: the need of research, no.69/70, «greg lynn – h2 house» & «greg lynn – embryo-building» (berlin: g & b arts international, december 1998/ january 1999), 46 -47 & 126-129. Daily telegraph (uk), «lively bricks: review of animate form» by l. bailey (thursday, 6th may 1999), 14. De architekt, «met het oog van de computer» (jaargang 30, november 1999), cover, 76-83. Die zeit (hamburg), «hausen in harmonie: greg lynn» by h. rauterberg (thursday, august 10, 2000). El croquis editorial, «forms of expression» and «interview with ben van berkel» (madrid, 1995). Financial times (london), «models give way to ideas» by a. rawsthorn (july 8, 2000). Figuras (revista de bolsillo sobre arquitectura): de las entrezonas y los deslugares «burujos. la medida de la complejidad & camandancia del puerto» (madrid, 1996). Hybrid space: new forms in digital architecture, edited by peter zellner (london: thames and hudson, 1999), 137-149. Hybrid space: new forms in digital architecture, greg lynn/form, los angeles (london: thames & hudson ltd., 1999), 136-149. Independent (uk), «cubes are good but the blobs are winning out,» by d. saatchi (sunday, june 25, 2000), 6-8. Interiors, « three for the show» ed. j. gray (march 2000) 19. Journal of philosophy and the visual arts, ed. a. benjamin, «body matters,» (london: academy group ltd., 1993), 60-69. Journal of philosophy and the visual arts: complexity, «blobs,» ed. a. benjamin, (london: academy group ltd., 1995), 39-44.

35

Lusitania: sites and stations, provisional utopias, (new york: june 1996), pps. 128-135. Metropolis magazine, «without a trace» by s. serifman (december 1998), 74-81. Metropolis magazine, «without a trace» by susanna serifman (december 1998), pps.74-81. Metropolis magazine, xx, metropolitan home magazine, xx. metropolitan home, «triple play» (march/april 2000) 84. New york magazine, «best bytes» j. giovannini (march 27, 2000) 32, 34, 36. New york magazine, «computing a cathedral» by k. jacobs (august 31, 1998), 44. New york magazine, «powers that will be: who will inherit n.y.?» by a. lange (december 21, 1998), 66. New york magazine, «cityscapes: computing a cathedral» by karrie jacobs (august 31, 1998), pp. 44. New york magazine, «the powers that will be: who will inherit new york?» by alexandra lange (december 21-28, 1998), pp. 66. New york newsday, «a grand design for a new church» by n. ruhling (monday, september 20, 1999), a23. New york newsday, «church revival» by c. murray (friday, october 3, 1997), re cover & c3. New york newsday, «church revival: neglected factory becoming foundation of house of worship» by caryn eve murray (friday, october 3, 1997), real estate cover – c3. Newsday, «a grand design for a new church» by nancy ruhling (monday, september 20, 1999), a23. Newsline, «afterwords and just in-time» (new york: columbia university gsapp, february 1992). Newsline, «complex variations» (new york: columbia university gsapp, september 1994). Newsline, «complexity & compliancy: shoei yoh's sports complex» (new york: columbia university gsapp, december 1992). Newsline, «peter eisenman informe» (new york: columbia university gsapp, february 1992). Parachute, «vers une architecture icarienne» interview with christine buci-glucksmann & « l'archietcture virtuelle: textures, paysages et cyborgs» by antoine picon (october, november & december 1999), 16-24 & 43-46. Pasajes, «coherencia en el cosmos o diagramas revestidos» by b. lootsma (no. 18) 18-26. Philip johnson: turning point, «the dynamics of surface» (vienna: springer verlage, 1997), pps. 8-12. Profile, no.21, «haus aus der datenbank» by roland kanfer (vienna, 22 may 1999), 150-151. Re: working eisenman, ed. a. benjamin, «ineffective descriptions: supplemental lines» (london: academy group ltd., 1993). Report: bau & immobilien, «mittels pc zum bau aus der bewegung» by jaan klasmann (november 1999), 40-44. Reversible destiny: arakawa and gins, «four architects on reversible destiny,» (new york: solomon r. guggenheim foundation, 1997), pps. 214-222. S.O.H. (states of humanity), «the architect» edited by alex vermeulen (antwerp: museum

of contemporary art (muhka), 1999). Slow space, «the parsing eye» by mark wamble (new york: monacelli press, 1998), 254-271. Space design, «cardiff bay opera house & cabrini green housing» (tokyo, september, 1994). Space design, shoei yoh: 12 calisthenics for architecture, «shoei yoh's movement from nature to a new vitalism» (tokyo, january, 1997), pps. 11-14. Space design, kengo kuma: digital gardening, «pointillism» (tokyo, 1997), pps. 46-47. Spectacular optical: catalogue, (new york: threadwaxing space, 1998). Sustainable architecture: towards a diverse built environment, by ed melet «visitors center omv, austrian mineral oil company, schwechat» (rotterdam: nai publishers, 1999), 144-147. The art of the accident, (rotterdam: nai publishers/v-2 organization, 1998). The daily telegraph (uk), «lively bricks: animate form (book and cd-rom) by liz bailey (thursday, 6th may 1999), 14. The japan architect, no.5, «comments on another glass house competition» (tokyo: shinkenchiku-sha co., ltd., 1992), 22-23. The los angeles times, «breaking down walls to houses of the future» by nicolai ouroussoff (wednesday, october 4, 2000), calendar section. The los angeles times, «the sacred and the mundane» by nicolai ouroussoff (sunday, august 1, 1999), c 59-60. The new york times, «architects grow reliant on the 40 – pound pencil: the computer» by e. taub (thursday, august 10, 2000) circuits, d 9. The new york times, «from a laundry to a church» by alan oser (sunday, july 28, 1996), re 7. The new york times, «1999 arts and leisure guide: architecture» by herbert muschamp (sunday, september 13, 1998), ar 121. The new york times, «a queens factory is born again, as a church» by herbert muschamp (sunday, september 5, 1999), ar 30. The new york times, «ideazapoppin': images fly at cooper-hewitt» herbert muschamp (friday, march 10, 2000) fal cover, 38. The new york times, «out of the ether, a new continent of art» by steven henry madoff (sunday, february 14, 1999), ar 37 & 40. The virtual architecture: «the difference between the possible and the impossible,» edited by ken sakamura & hiroyuki suzuki, (tokyo: tokyo digital museum, 1997), pps. 128-133. Time magazine, «visions 21 – what will our skyline look like?» by richard lacayo (february 21, 2000) 80-82. Time magazine, innovators time 100: the next wave, «the look of the new,» by r. lacayo, (july 17, 2000) 64. Trans architecture, (tokyo 1998), pps. 61-86. Trans, «convertible vehicles» by jordan crandall, vol. 1/2, issue 3/4 (new york, 1997), 29-37. Trans: spectacular optical exhibition catalogue (new york: trans, 1998). Wallpaper, «venice biennale review,» (september 2000). Weiderhall 16: towards a supple geometry, «ineffective descriptions: supplemental lines» (amsterdam: idea books, 1994).

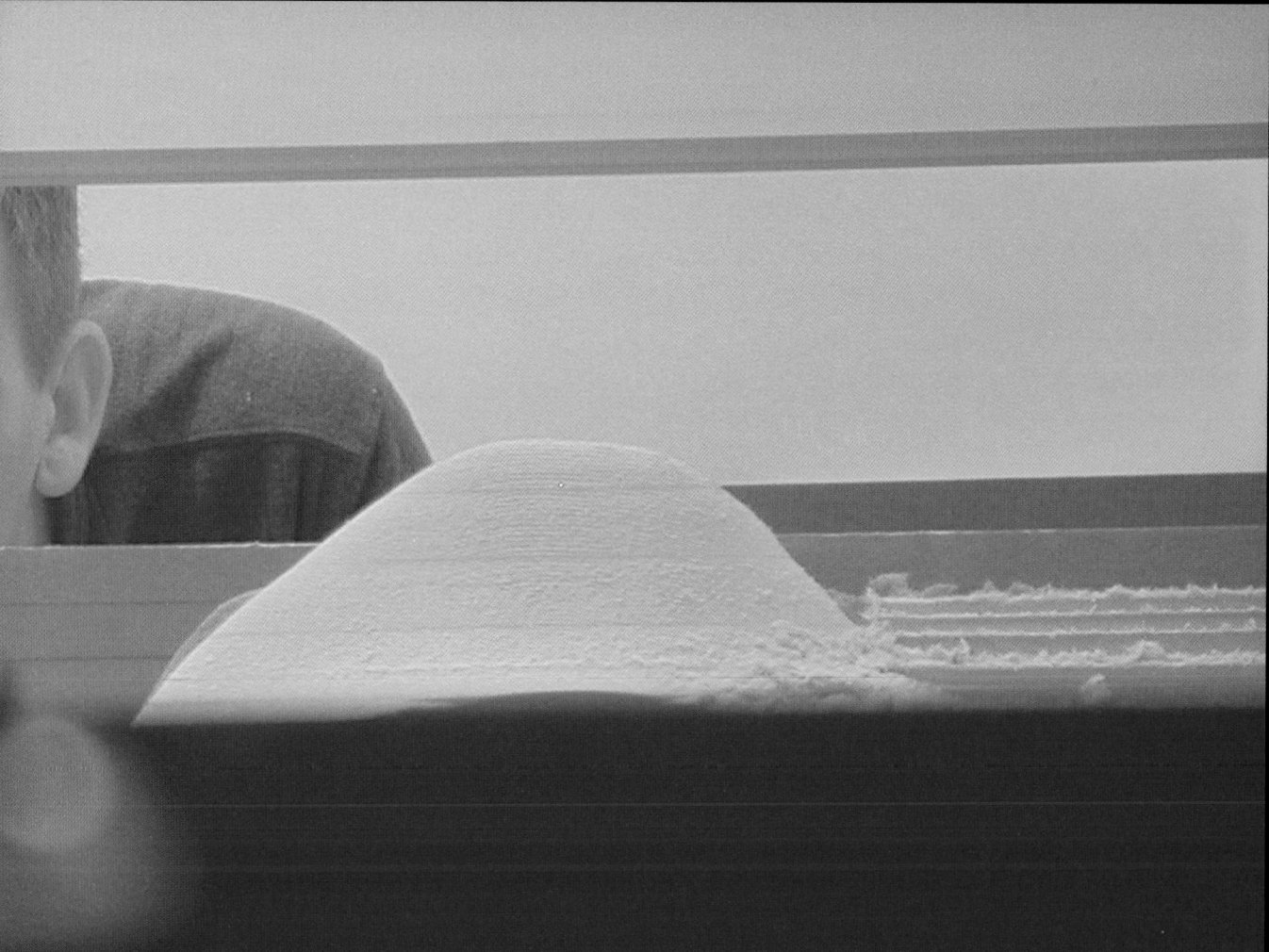

die gäste *the guests*

tokujin yoshioka

tokujin yoshioka, tokyo

«design»
als designer versuche ich, in jedem projekt eine neue herausforderung zu sehen. Aufgrund dieser herausforderung, neue möglichkeiten zu erschließen, entwickle ich ideen, die innovativ sind und sich vom herkömmlichen absetzen. Für mich bedeutet das wort «design» etwas, das neue, zukunftsträchtige werte schafft, gleichzeitig aber auch gefühle ausdrückt wie erstaunen, freude und rührung.

    ich zögere, einige ausdrucksformen unter dem namen design zu subsumieren. Darunter gehören auch solche, die bloß selbstgefällig sind, die nur auf mode oder vergangenem basieren, deren einzige absicht es ist, anzugeben.

«design»
as a designer, for each project, i try my best to approach a new challenge. And through this challenge of searching for the new possibilities, i come up with ideas which are novel and depart from the conventional. For me, the word «design» is a word which creates a new value leading on to the future, as well as expressing emotions such as surprise, joy, and being touched.

    i hesitate to classify some expressions under the name of design. These include those which are merely self-satisfactory, those which are based only on fashion or examples from the past, and those where the sole purpose is only to show off.

grundsätzlich glaube ich, daß design in der freien entfaltung der phantasie für die zukunft entstehen soll. Es ist mir ein besonderes anliegen, ein design zu kreieren, das ich selbst bisher noch nie gesehen habe, aber sehen möchte. Denn in mir schlummert der wunsch, mich und andere zu überraschen. Ich messe mich daran, ob ich ein design schaffen kann, das menschen rührt und erstaunt. Ich hoffe ferner, ein design zu liefern, das möglichst klar und perfekt ist.

kinder betrachten objekte intuitiv. Dementsprechend bedeutet die aussage, «das ist klar», eher eine gefühlsmäßige überzeugung, die keiner erklärung bedarf. Wahrscheinlich ist das etwas, das im wahrsten sinne ohne zu denken begriffen werden kann. Manche sagen, daß meine designobjekte ähnlichkeit mit den installationen der gegenwartskunst haben, und wahrscheinlich ist das so, weil ich diese ideen schätze. Das zweite kriterium, die perfektion des designs, zielt auf akzeptanz durch die fachwelt. Wenn diese beiden ziele erreicht sind, wird das objekt höchstwahrscheinlich ein erfolg sein und alle betrachter bewegen.

basically, i believe that design should be created for the future with free imagination. I strongly hope to create a design which i myself have never seen, and which i want to see. Because in me, there is a desire to surprise myself and others. Therefore, one of the standards by which i assess myself is whether i can create a design which touches and amazes people. And i hope to provide a design which is as clear and on as high a level as possible.

children look at objects intuitively. Similar to this, when one says «it's clear», that means being able to «feel» it even without explanation. Perhaps it is a thing which one reaches one's hand out for without thinking. Some say that my designs have a similarity with installations in contemporary art, and maybe that is because i value these ideas highly. The other element, of design having to be of a high level, is so that it is accepted by professionals as well. When these two aims are achieved, the design is very likely to be a success where everyone can be touched.

das aber zu erreichen, scheint das schwierigste überhaupt zu sein. Je schlichter die gestaltung, desto notwendiger wird es, darüber lange und genau nachzudenken. Vielleicht ist das so eine sache wie mit der japanischen küche. Verglichen mit der westlichen küche scheint die japanische sehr einfach zu sein. Wie viel zeit auch während des zubereitungsprozesses aufgewendet werden muss, am gericht scheint man das nicht zu merken. Wenn man es dann aber gekostet hat, begreift man das können des küchenchefs. Einfache ergebnisse mit einfachen prozessen gleichzusetzen trifft auf die japanische küche nicht zu: ähnliches gilt hoffentlich auch für meine gestaltungsarbeit.

however, it also seems that to achieve this is the most difficult thing. The simpler the design is, the more necessary it becomes to think deeply and carefully about it. Perhaps it is just like japanese cuisine. Compared to western cuisine, japanese cuisine appears to be very simple. No matter how much time and effort is spent during the cooking process, the cuisine itself does not seem to show much trace of it. Yet once it is tasted, one realises the chef's expertise. The equation of the result being simple and the process not being simple does not apply to japanese cuisine, and i aspire to design similarly.

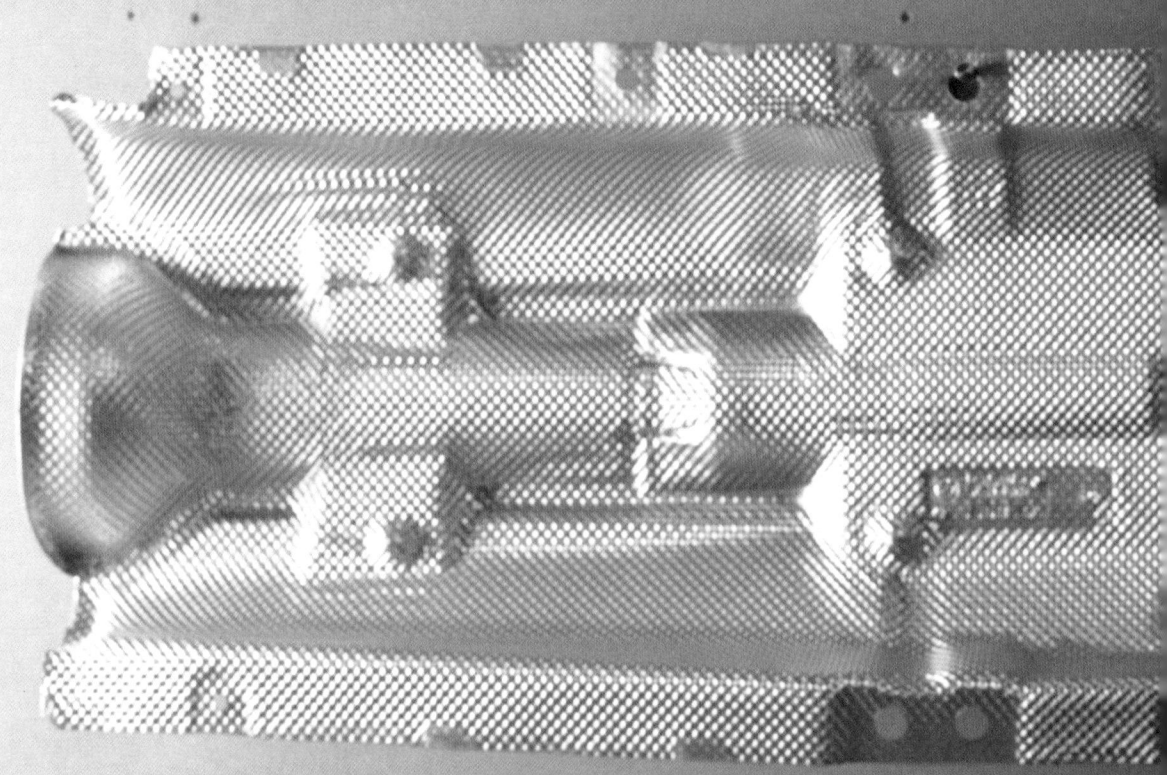

«expanding the gap»
ich habe versucht, die lücke zu erweitern, indem ich ein natürliches phänomen in diesem raum gestaltet habe. Mit dieser installation wollte ich nicht nur die lücke erweitern, sondern auch die erinnerung der menschen freisetzen, indem ich die grenze zwischen zeit und raum aufzulösen versuchte. Auf diese weise, so glaube ich, stellt sie einen unbegrenzten raum dar.

für dieses schneebild dachten wir darüber nach, wie der schnee am schönsten fallen könnte. Der schnee besteht aus federn, die, von einem ventilator aufgewirbelt, einen schneesturm über köln auslösen. Ich glaube, daß ich in der lage war, die menschen zu berühren und ihnen das staunen zu vermitteln.

«expanding the gap»
by designing the phenomena of nature, i tried to «expand the gap» within this space. In this installation, not only did i try to «expand the gap», but i wanted to trigger people's memories by doing so: i wanted it to remove the boundary between time and space. This way, i believe it expresses an unlimited amount of space.

    in this «snow-image», we thought how to make the snow fall beautifully. The snow is made out of feathers and by blowing it up with a fan, we could make it snow in cologne. I believe i was able to touch people and give them a sense of wonderment.

weitere beiträge *further contributions*

köbi gantenbein

köbi gantenbein, zürich

«expanding the gap» oder wie ein schweizer bergbub mit bildern die weite sucht und feststellt, daß da, wo er wohnt, die fremden die weite und das weite zu finden hoffen, das sie schon so lange suchen. Ein beitrag zur bergfotografie und zur erforschung der weitsicht.

«expanding the gap», or how a lad from the swiss mountains searches for faraway places in pictures and finds out that where he lives is where foreigners hope to find the broad expanses they have been looking for for so long. A comment on mountain photography and a contribution to research in far-sightedness.

der zug der linie landquart-davos hatte den tunnel beim fuchsenwinkel im prättigau verlassen, als die kleine clara ladner schon am bahnbord wartete. Gemächlich rottelten die vier personen- und der gepäckwagen, gezogen von der dampflokomotive mit dem stolzen namen «heidi», gegen jenaz. Clara ladner war meine großmutter und sie erzählte mir von ihrer frühen liebe zu den zügen, die damals erst seit ein paar jahren durchs prättigau gegen davos fuhren. Sie war sieben jahre alt, als hans castorp, gerädert von der 24 stunden langen reise von hamburg nach davos auf den «zauberberg», auch in einem solchen zug gesessen haben mußte. Hielt castorp, froh um etwas frische luft, das fenster seines abteils offen? Hat er sich etwas gestreckt und zum fenster hinaus geschaut? Dann hat er gewiß clara ladner gesehen. Hat er meiner großmutter zugewinkt?

    ich glaube nicht. Denn wenn ich, jahre nachdem wir meine großmutter auf den friedhof getragen haben, seine abenteuer in davos lese, weiß ich, daß er es eher mit all den anderen fremden hielt. Man blieb unter sich. Er versteckte sich auf der fahrt hinter dem grünen vorhänglein in seinem coupé, er war froh, wenn der zug endlich über den wolfgangpaß fuhr und spedierte sich und seinen großen koffer schnurstracks ins sanatorium auf dem zauberberg. Und auch

the train on the landquart-davos line had only just left the fuchsenwinkel tunnel in prättigau, and little clara ladner was already waiting on the platform. Unhurriedly, the steam locomotive proudly bearing the name «heidi» chugged towards jenaz, drawing its four carriages and baggage car. Clara ladner was my grandmother, and she told me how much she had loved trains when they had only been running through the prättigau valley in the direction of davos for a few years. She was seven years old when hans castorp, exhausted from the 24 hour journey from hamburg to the «magic mountain» in davos, must have sat in a train like that. Did castorp keep the window of his compartment open, happy to breathe some fresh air? Did he stretch a little and gaze out of the window? If he did, he would have been sure to see clara ladner. Did he wave to my grandmother?

    i think not. For when i read of his adventures in davos, years after my grandmother was carried to her grave, i know that he will have done just the same as all the other strangers. They keep themselves to themselves. During the journey, he hid behind the little green curtain in his compartment, was happy when the train finally scaled the wolfgangpass, and had himself and his large case con-

später verzehrte er sich lieber nach madame aus rußland, als daß er hinter einer gesunden davoserin hergewesen wäre, und lieber hörte er settembrini zu, statt daß er mit einem guler, gredig oder jost über seine geplanten ausflüge gesprochen und ihnen zumindest einen verdienst als bergführer gegeben hätte.

mit schadenfreude denke ich daran, wie er sich meist verirrt hat. Die einheimischen berge haben ihn ab und zu interessiert, die einheimischen menschen nicht. Er suchte das weite und stolperte über wurzeln. Die, die da wohnten und lebten, waren allenfalls gut als diener auf der etage, pferdeknechte in den stallungen und mägde in den großen unterirdischen kellern, wasch- und garküchen. Einmal widmete er sich ihnen und unterschob, sie würden «straßenfasching» feiern, was sie in davos um 1907 aber mit garantie nicht getan haben. Fasnacht treiben da auch heute nur die fremden. Castorps und seinesgleichen bild über die bereisten war verschwommen, sein interesse herablassend. Bei rousseau hatten sie es besser. Er war der große porträtist derer, die da wohnten, und illumierte sie so, daß sie als folie brauchbar waren für die reichen in den städten, die mit wundem herzen auf das weite hofften.

veyed speedily straight to the sanatorium on the magic mountain. Later, too, he preferred to pine for madame from russia rather than pursue one of the healthy maids of davos, and preferred to listen to settembrini rather than addressing a word about his planned excursions to a guler, gredig or jost and at least providing them with an obolus for service as a mountain guide.

i think with a wry smile how often he was wrong. The local mountains interested him from time to time; the local people not at all. He searched for broad expanses, and stumbled over roots. The people who lived and worked there were just good enough to be floor waiters, stable boys and maids in the huge subterranean cellars, kitchens and wash-houses. Once, his gaze alighted upon them and he assumed they were celebrating a «street carnival», which they most certainly would not have done in davos in 1907. Even today, carnival there is for the visitors only. Castorp's view of the visited, like that of his kind, was blurred, and his interest condescending. With rousseau they had it better. He was the great portrait painter of those who lived there, and illuminated them in such a way that they could serve as foils to the rich in the cities who longed with bleeding hearts for broad, empty expanses.

dieses bild hat sich nicht verändert, seit clara ladner am bahndamm stand, und den sechziger jahren des letzten jahrhunderts, in denen ich, ihr enkel, in ihr alter kam. Es war brauch, daß unsereins in den schulferien an «eine stelle» ging. Ich durfte zurück nach samedan, einem ort bei st. moritz, wo ich auf die welt gekommen war, und ich war gast bei familie muggli.

    zusammen mit silvali, meiner ersten großen liebe, wurde ich caddy auf dem golfplatz. Wir trugen den golfern die säcke nach, für die gebrechlichen mußten wir das kleine plastikstücklein in den rasen stecken und den ball darauf plazieren. Wenn sie die bälle in den teich schossen, mußten wir sie herausholen. Herr stoffel, unser meister, hatte es uns strengstens verboten, mit der kundschaft zu sprechen oder ihr in die augen zu sehen. Am schluß gab es ein trinkgeld.

    viele jahre später knorzte ich an meiner diplomarbeit als soziologe über die bilderwelt des tourismus. Wie ein blitz schlug ein plakat aus samedan in meine zu erforschende grundgesamtheit von 458 plakaten ein: eine reizende dame in weiß mit hut und bubikopf, ein soldatischer herr in braunen knickerbockers mit tabakpfeife, links im bild ein kleiner bub in kurzen hosen, roten socken und genagelten schuhen, der den herrschaften einen golfschläger reicht. Gesichter

this picture has not changed at all since clara ladner stood on the platform, or since the sixties of the last century in which i, her grandson, reached the age she was then. It was the custom for us, in the school holidays, to take up a «position». I was permitted to return to samedan, a village by st. moritz, where i had first seen the light of the world, and was put up by the muggli family.

    together with silvali, my first love, i became a caddy on the golf course. We followed the golfers with their bags, and for the infirm we had to push the little pieces of plastic into the ground and place the balls upon them. When they drove the balls into the pond, we had to fish them out. Mr stoffel, our master, had strictly forbidden us to talk to the clients or look them straight in the eye. At the end, there were tips.

    many years later, i was struggling with my degree thesis in sociology on the pictorial world of tourism. Like lightning, a poster from samedan flashed out from my accumulated totality of 458: a charming lady in white with bobbed hair and a hat, a military-looking gentleman in brown knickerbockers with a pipe, and at the left in the picture a little boy in short trousers, red socks and hobnailed shoes, handing a golf club to the gentlefolk. Only the latter have

haben nur die herrschaften, der knabe hat keines. Dafür trägt er auf dem kopf einen großen hut und eine feder: der kleine indianer war ich. Und mich faszinierte die fremde sprache der fremden, die zu uns kamen um die weite des herzens mit der weite der bergen zu messen, und ich fragte mich mehr als einmal: wann wird mich ein mister mitnehmen, vielleicht gar mit dem schiff übers meer?

fünf jahre später fand ich als zwölfjähriger «meine stelle» auf der lenzerheide im grandhotel schweizerhof. Den ersten teil des sommers hatte ich in der küche zu helfen, heiße pfannen putzen zusammen mit einem portugiesen, der über einen mächtigen schwarzen schnauz verfügte und mich, die bratenresten schrubbend, theoretisch und endgültig mit den geheimnissen der frau bekannt machte. Im zweiten teil meiner hotelkarriere stieg ich, weil ich spurenweise französisch und englisch konnte, zum stellvertreter des spanischen bademeisters auf, obschon ich nichtschwimmer war. Da wollte ich die kenntnisse, die ich im küchenverlies gehört hatte, praktisch an damen anwenden.

    ihr bild hatte mich schon auf den plakaten in der hotelhalle betört. Mich faszinierte, wie die bildermacher der berge die damen immer mit dem blick ins weite darstellten

faces; the boy has none. Instead, he is wearing a large hat with a feather: that little indian was me. I was also fascinated by the strange language of the strangers who came to us to measure the breadth of their hearts against the breadth of the mountains, and i wondered more than once: when will one of these misters take me with him, perhaps even on a ship across the sea?

five years later, when i was twelve, i took up my «position» at the grand hotel schweizerhof in the lenzerheide. The first part of the summer was spent helping in the kitchen, washing hot pans together with a portuguese who sported a massive black moustache and, scrubbing away at the remains of roasts, theoretically and conclusively initiated me into the mysteries of the female sex. In the second part of my hotel career i rose, on account of my traces of french and english, to be deputy to the spanish bath attendant, although i could not swim. There, i planned to put the theory i had heard in my kitchen dungeon into practice with the ladies.

    their pictures on the posters in the hotel lobby had already infatuated me. I was fascinated by how the portraitists of the mountains always showed the ladies gazing

und diese also in ihrem traum abholen. Das interesse der damen aus der weiten welt an mir aber war ganz und gar lau. Aufgrund meiner erfahrungen glaubte ich dem österreichischen koch, der mit mir und fünf andern das zimmer im personalhaus teilte, kein wort, wenn er davon schwärmte, was er und die ältere tochter der noblen französischen familie von tisch fünf in seiner zimmerstunde jeweils miteinander anstellten. Er war von seiner arbeit in der küche käsebleich, ich konnte wenigstens eine gewisse berglerbräune vorzeigen. Auch habe ich ihn ertappt, wie er mit sich selber anstellte, was er mit der noblen französin anzustellen vorgab.

glücklicherweise hatte ich dafür kurz darauf die praktische gelegenheit, den theorieunterricht des portugiesen mit der tochter eines gastwirts, die es ebenfalls auf an eine «stelle» in den schweizerhof verschlagen hatte, zu versuchen. Und etwas später vertiefte eine studentin aus wien, die als serviertochter wirkte, das eben geübte mit mir und führte mich, es war 1970, gleichzeitig in die mir vollkommen neue weite welt von karl marx ein. Kurz und gut: die beziehungen im tourismus sind klar geregelt und die sozialen und kulturellen schranken funktionieren im paradies noch viel stärker als

into the distance, catching them in the middle of their dreams. but the interest the ladies of the world showed in me was luke-warm, if that. With the benefit of my experience, i believed nothing of what the austrian chef, who shared the room in the staff lodgings with me and five others, told me when he enthused about the goings on between him and the elder daughter of the noble french family from table five during his hour off. He was as pale as cheese from his work in the kitchen, and i at least could show off a certain mountaineering tan. Also, i once caught him doing with himself what he pretended to have been doing with the aristocratic young frenchwoman.

luckily, i had a practical opportunity to test the portuguese's theory shortly afterwards with a publican's daughter who had also been sent off to a «position» in the schweizerhof. Somewhat later, a student from vienna, who was acting as a serving maid, deepened my newly acquired knowledge and at the same time – it was 1970 – introduced me to the totally new world of karl marx. To put it in a nutshell, the relationships in tourism are clearly regulated, and the social and cultural barriers function even more effectively in paradise than outside it. The

außerhalb. Die bereisten erfahren die welt, das glück und die zuversicht unter sich. Und den reisenden ist diese form der abschottung durchaus auch recht. Nur sich mit einem geißenpeter fotografieren zu lassen, gehört allenfalls zum programm, das man zurück aus der weite, in der stadt dokumentiert haben will.

    diese einsicht verstärkte sich, als ich ein paar jahre später touristisch aufsteigen konnte und als gymnasiast dank der sprachkenntnisse skilehrer wurde. Die blaue jacke mit den gelben streifen erwies sich nicht als schlüssel in die zimmer der fremden, schönen frauen, die mit pelzmänteln flanierten und filmgeruch aus der weiten welt verströmten, wohin unsereins unbedingt wollte. Auch wenn ich die jacke abends in der stickend heißen bar getragen habe und mir dabei fast schlecht wurde, half sie dem erotischen fortkommen nicht. Selbst in den mir zugeteilten klassen brauchte ich viel balzarbeit und plagieren als leidlich guter skifahrer bis ich, nach einigen schmerzvollen abschiffern, endlich bei der amerikanischen medizinstudentin linda landen konnte. Amerika! New york – war sie der schlüssel in die weite welt?

    sie hatte sich aber in mich als person verliebt, mein ganzes einheimischenschicksal war ihr egal. Linda ging ohne

visited experience the world, happiness and confidence among themselves, and the visitors find that form of segregation thoroughly acceptable. Only having themselves photographed with peter the goatherd is a compulsory part of the programme which, on one's return from foreign parts, has to be documented.

    this insight became even more acute when i rose further in the tourism industry a few years later and, thanks to my knowledge of languages, became a skiing instructor. The blue jacket with the yellow stripes proved not to be the key to the rooms of those beautiful women from distant parts who lounged about in fur coats and exuded the scent of a faraway film industry where we all wanted to be, whatever the cost. Even when i wore the jacket in the chokingly hot bar of an evening and almost fainted doing so, it failed to aid my erotic progress. And even in the classes assigned to me i needed to do a lot of sweet talking and posing as a tolerably good skier until, after a number of painful put-downs, i finally made it with american medical student linda. America! New york! Was she the key to the wide world?

    but she had fallen in love with me as a person, and was utterly indifferent to my fate as a local. Linda

mich aufs flugzeug. Ich war natürlich unter uns kollegen keine ausnahme. Wir bändelten mit skilehrerkolleginnen an. Ich entflammte für annabarbara, eine bauerntochter. Und selbst kurt, uns als doktorsohn immer einen schritt voraus, der charmant und grade heraus verfolgte, was wir andern eher mit kurven versuchten, selbst kurt verstrickte sich in eine dramatische affäre mit einer einheimischen, nachdem es mit den engländerinnen nicht so recht funken schlagen mochte. Und peter, der einzige, der es zu veritablen bergführerehren brachte, heiratete schnurstracks eine einheimische. Kurz – auch als skilehrer, im zenit des heldenbildes vom tourismusprospekt und der bergfotografie, war es nicht anders als als caddy, als casserolier oder als vizebademeister. Die fremde war schwierig zu erreichen, das weite weit weg. Die einheimischen blieben unter sich. Und letztlich taten beide gut daran, denn sonst wäre ich jetzt vielleicht in new york und somit zu weit weg vom kanton graubünden und den bergen.

weshalb ist das so? Ist es die rauhe sprache der bergler, ist es die soziale struktur und die klassenbildung, hatten wir insgeheim angst wegen zuviel kontakts mit den fremden, unsere familien verlassen zu müssen? Bin ich gar nicht

embarked on the plane without me. I was, of course, no exception among my colleagues. We flirted with the skiing instructresses, and i developed a burning passion for annabarbara, a farmer's daughter. Even kurt, always one step ahead of us as a doctor's son, charmingly going straight for what we others still meandered about, even kurt became entangled in a dramatic affair with one of the local maids when the spark had failed to spring across to the english girls. And peter, the only one of us who actually became a fully-fledged mountain guide, married one of the locals straight off. In short, even as a skiing instructor, at the zenith of heroism as presented by the tourist brochures and mountain photographs, things were no different from what they had been as a caddy, a dish-washer or a deputy bath attendant. The foreign girls were hard to get, and the distant world remained out of reach. The locals stayed amongst themselves. And just as well for both of them in the end, for otherwise i might be in new york now, too far away from the canton of graubünden and the mountains.

why is that so? is it the rough speech of the mountain folk, is it the social structure and the class system, and did we

geeignet, das weite zu suchen und zu finden? Ich habe solche fragen lange jahre mit mir getragen und sie schließlich in meiner abschlußarbeit als soziologe an der universität gestellt. Die antwort versteckt sich, wie es sich gehört, hinter einem bedeutenden titel: «tourismus als veranstaltung und regime. Eine geschichte des tourismusplakat und der bergfotografie im kanton graubünden». Neben der erfindung der bündner landschaft, neben der karriere der bergbahnen und autostraßen vom lieblingsmotiv zu dem, was man, je mehr man hat, um so weniger zeigt, neben dem verschwinden der erotik aus den plakatbildern, weil die mittelständler-familien sich in den vierziger jahren in die berge aufmachten – neben all diesen nebensächlichkeiten habe ich ein kapitel dem bild des einheimischen auf dem tourismusplakat gewidmet.

und nun steht wissenschaftlich hieb- und stichfest und mit guter note belegt fest: die reklamemacher malen verbal und visuell ein dem fortkommen der bergler ungünstiges bild. Wir dürfen nicht ins weite, denn wir sind dazu geboren, dort kulissen zu schieben, wohin die fremden kommen, um, ausbrechend aus ihrer enge, in den engen bergen das weite zu suchen. Wir, die einheimischen, tauchen, verteilt in 458 plakaten über 83 jahre, nur in stabilen rollen und berufen

have too much contact with the strangers, making us secretly fear to leave our families? am i just incapable of seeking and finding space? i carried those questions around with me for years, and finally asked them in my degree thesis in sociology at the university. The answer was hidden, as is fitting and proper, behind a weighty title: «tourism as event and regime. A history of the tourism poster and mountain photography in canton graubünden.» together with the invention of the bünden landscape, together with the career of the mountain railways and roads from favourite motifs to what is shown less the more one has of it, together with the disappearance of the erotic from the posters because middle class families started invading the mountains in the forties – together with all these incidentals, i dedicated a chapter to the image of the locals on tourism posters.

now, therefore, it has been scientifically established beyond a shadow of doubt and sealed with a good grade: verbally and visually, the advertisers paint a picture which is unconducive to progress on the part of the mountain folk. We are not allowed to venture out to faraway places, for we are born to be scene-shifters where the strangers come, breaking out of their strait-laced cities to seek the

auf: fünf skilehrer und bergführer, vier kellner, drei kutscher, drei golfcaddies, zwei bauern, zwei bauernbuben, zwei bäuerinnen, eine bauerntochter, ein chauffeur, ein rhb-kondukteur und eine serviertochter. Die soziale beziehung folgt zwei mustern: dienender blick und fröhliches, aber beziehungsloses lachen richtung plakatrand oder himmel.

viel wichtiger als die bereisten sind die reisenden, die von zuhause weg gehen und gegen geld in den bergen das weite und die weite suchen. Ihre bilder zeigen lebensglück, muße und beziehungsvielfalt je nach epochen und sozialer vorliebe. Sind die einheimischen immer allein mit ihrem blick, so treten die reisenden am liebsten in situationen vor oder nach der paarung auf. Durchwegs lachen sie ein einander an, in den zwanziger jahren der erotische blick der ledigen auf abenteuertour in den bergen. Schon in den dreißiger jahren wird's je nach kurort züchtig. Der tourismus will nun auch die familien aus dem mittelstand, und statt dame im bubikopf kommen mammi, papi und kind aufs bild. Reich und modern ist man alleweil, man tanzt, man spielt, man speist und hat schöne kleider. Und tritt aus dem alltagsleben in die weite welt des luxus. Das ganze schauspiel hat ja schon hans castorp vorgeführt mit seinen ewigen auf- und abtritten im speisesaal des sanatoriums. Und was als sport-

freedom of the mountains. We, the locals, spread over 458 posters spanning 83 years, only appear in stable roles and professions: five skiing instructors and mountain guides, four waiters, three coachmen, three golf caddies, two farmers, two farmer's boys, two farmer's wives, one farmer's daughter, one chauffeur, one train conductor and a serving maid. The social relationships follow two patterns: a servile glance, and a happy but detached smile directed at the edge of the poster or the sky.

the visitors, who leave their homes and pay money to disappear into the mountains and search for space, are much more important than their hosts. Their pictures display happy lives, leisure and a variety of relationships, depending on the epoch and social preferences. While the locals are always alone with their distracted gazes, the tourists appear predominantly in situations before or after mating. They smile at each other throughout, in the twenties with the erotic glances of singles on an adventure tour in the mountains. In the thirties, chastity already supervenes at several health resorts. The tourist trade now wants the families from the middle classes, and the lady with bobbed hair is replaced in the picture by mummy and daddy and baby. They are still rich and modern: dancing,

lich, jung, attraktiv gilt, verändert sich über all die jahre nicht. Der tourismus hat einen stabilen fröhlichen weitsichtmenschen erfunden.

doch das bild der die weite und das weite suchenden reisenden auf der bergfotografie verändert sich laufend. Sie tun mir fast leid. Meistens sind sie allein auf dem bergfoto und hektisch mit irgend einer sportlichen tat beschäftigt: hechtspringen vor alpenkulisse, kopfüber vom skeleton stürzen, bob fahren im sommer, velorasen im militärkostüm, verzweifelt ein boot steuern, einsam durch die luft fallen oder wettbrüllen. Oft schauen die feriengäste mich mit verzerrtem blick an, lachen nur, weil sie von der reklameagentur geld dafür erhalten und dann leicht irr. Und – die armen sind meistens allein mit sich und ihrer anstrengung. Endlich ferien. Das heißt übersetzt, ich kämpfe mit mir gegen mich. Wo sind die großen diners der plakatbilder und des zauberbergs? Wo die knisternden aufrisse der zwanziger jahre? Wo die weite des abendrots? Wo die ausländische dame, die mich aus dem bild heraus so anlachte, daß ich als vizebademeister unruhig wurde? Wo die sommernacht à deux? Wo die traute familie im glück in den bergen, umgeben von pflanzen, tieren und gesunder luft? Und so bleibt nur die

gambling, dining and beautifully dressed. Leaving everyday life behind and entering the wide world of luxury. Of course, the whole performance has already been presented by hans castorp with his eternal entrances and exits in the dining room at the sanatorium. What is regarded as athletic, young and attractive remains the same through all those years. Tourism has invented stable, cheery, farsighted man.

but the picture in mountain photography of the travellers seeking this distance and space changes constantly. I am almost sorry for them. In most cases, they are alone on the photo, and hectically coping with one sporting feat or another: jack-knifing against the backdrop of the alps, diving head first from the skeleton, bob sleighing in the summer, racing on bicycles in military costume, desperately steering a boat, dropping alone through the air or roaring away in a shouting contest. Often, the holidaymakers look at me with a contorted gaze, only laugh because they are paid to do so by the advertising agency, and then slightly madly. And these poor people are mostly alone with themselves and their efforts. Holidays at last. That means fighting with yourself. Where are the great dinners of the

schlußfolgerung: tourismus ist anstrengend geworden. Die weite bleibt ein traum, reisender sein ein harter beruf. Die ferienarbeit ist um nichts weniger entfremdet als die normale. Vielleicht ist es aber auch ganz anders und die bergfotografen der gegenwart leisten abbitte an ihren vorfahren, die uns bereisten seinerzeit so prüfungsreiche wege bereitet haben.

posters and the magic mountain? Where are the sizzling prospects of the twenties? Where, the breadth of the sunset? Where, the foreign lady smiling at me, the deputy bath attendant, so disturbingly from the picture? Where are the summer nights à deux? Where, the cosy, happy family in the mountains, surrounded by flora, fauna and healthy air? There can be only one conclusion: tourism has become an effort. Over the hills and far away remains a dream, and travelling is a hard occupation. Holiday work is no less alienating than a normal job. Perhaps, though, it is all quite different and the mountain photographers of the present are begging forgiveness for their forerunners who blazed such trails full of ordeals for us, the visited.

köbi gantenbein arbeitet als chefredaktor von hochparterre, der schweizer zeitschrift für gestaltung und architektur. Er ist im engadin geboren und im prättigau aufgewachsen, spricht walserdialekt und wohnt in der stadt zürich. All das liegt in der schweiz. Er blickt auf eine spannende karriere als bewohner der enge zurück, war golfcaddy, casserolier, vizebademeister, hilfsskilehrer, hotelportier, ländlerklarinettist und kellner im speisewagen chur – st. moritz. Später studierte er an der universität zürich soziologie und geschichte und schloß sein diplom mit einer arbeit über die geschichte des tourismusplakats in graubünden von 1900 bis 1983 ab. Damit bewältigte er seine prüfungen als bereister knabe und jüngling und fand – befreite seele – den weg in die weite welt.

köbi gantenbein is the editor in chief of hochparterre, the magazine for design and architecture. He was born in engadin and grew up in prättigau, speaks walser dialect and lives in the city of zurich. All of that is in switzerland. He can look back on an exciting career as an inhabitant of that narrow world: he was a golf caddy, dish-washer, deputy bath attendant, assistant skiing instructor, hotel porter, folk music clarinettist and waiter in the chur – st. moritz dining car. Later, he studied sociology and history at the university of zurich, taking his degree with a thesis on the history of tourism posters in graubünden from 1900 to 1983. Thus he survived his ordeals as a boy and youth in the world of the visitors and, a liberated soul, found his way into the wide world.

weitere beiträge *further contributions*

hannes heer

hannes heer, hamburg

«auch togo bleibt deutsch»

ein beitrag über den witz auf dem marsch oder wie der spaß ein loch in die wand schlägt – vier jahre, bevor die bundesregierung die oder-neiße-linie als deutsch-polnische grenze anerkannte und willy brandts kniefall am denkmal des warschauer-ghetto-aufstandes eine neue epoche einleitete.

«give togo back to the germans»

a contribution about the joke on the march or how fun punches a hole in the wall – four years before the federal government recognized the oder-neisse line as the german-polish border and willi brandt's genuflection at the memorial of the warsaw ghetto revolt rang in a new epoch.

die drei männer blicken ihn an. Der eine breitschultrig, im dunklen sommerjanker mit offenem schillerkragen, ein massiger kopf mit zurückfliehendem haar, er weicht keinem kampf aus, lauert darauf, die augen schlitze, die pranken noch seitwärts hängend. Hinter ihm mit bürstenschnitt über hoher stirn, hornbrille, schlips, leichter mantel, die kamera um den hals, halboffener mund, der demagoge, sie da, was sie da sagen unerhört. Vorne grinst der dritte, kahlköpfig im verschwitzten sakko, eine böse gemütlichkeit, warte wir kommen.

dann die frau, eine nike von irgendwo, hoch den kopf über der gestärkten bluse, zusammengekniffene augen, verächtlich der mund, das gesicht gegen den feind. Im schlepptau zwei mißtrauische alte mit vogelfederhut und 20er-jahre-frisur, an der seite ein kräftiger greis mit ekelriechendem kaltem stumpen. Ein transparent, auf dem angedroht wird, daß jemand über eine denkschrift richten wird. Auf einem andern läßt sich entziffern: heimatrecht.

the three men look at him. One with broad shoulders, in a dark summer jacket covered by an open shirt collar, a bulky head with hair flowing back: a man not to shrink from a fight, lying in wait, the eyes slits and huge paws still dangling at his sides. Behind him, with a crew cut over a high forehead, horn-rimmed glasses, a tie, lightweight coat, camera around his neck and mouth half open, the demagogue, hey you, what you're saying is outrageous. at the front, the third one grins, bald-headed in a sweatstained jacket, exuding an evil congeniality, just wait, we're coming.

then the woman, a nike from somewhere or other, head carried high over the starched blouse, eyes screwed half shut, a contemptuous mouth, face turned towards the enemy. Following in her wake, two mistrustful old women with a feather hat and 1920s hairstyles, and at the side a robust old man with a foul-smelling unlit cigar butt. A banner threatening someone's judgement on a memorandum.

der platz, voll gedrängt mit menschen. Transparente. Eine kundgebung. Commerzbank, sternhotel, apotheke, ein breiter treppenaufgang. Zum ersten mal erkennt er etwas – der platz vor dem bonner rathaus. Die stadtfahne am mast, daneben der schriftzug oppeln. Im hintergrund an einem kaufhaus: aktuelle freizeitmoden. Sonst fragmente: ostdeutsches land vor dem untergang. Der schlesier. Alles andere unleserlich, überbelichtet. Selbst die lachenden männer verdecken noch die aufschriften. Irgendetwas triumphiert könnte der dicke im kurzärmeligen hemd buchstabieren.

andere transparente. Pappe roh auf dachlatten genagelt. In den grenzen von 800. Er erkennt sich auf dem foto, das lachen, die starken zähne, das bügelfreie nyltesthemd mit der einzigen krawatte, die er besaß, die billige kassenbrille. Rechts hinter ihm sein freund bernd r. Verlorenen krieg kann er lesen. Dann nur noch fragmente. Ein großes m. Die endsilbe itz. Alles dieselbe machart. Daneben befestigen andere

on another, the right to a homeland can just be made out.

the square, pulsating with people. Banners. A political rally. The commerzbank, sternhotel, a chemist's shop and a broad staircase. For the first time he recognises something – the square in front of the city hall in bonn. The city flag flying from its pole, and next to it the lettering, oppeln. In the background, on a department store: latest casual wear. Otherwise, fragments: east german territory facing ruin. The silesian. Everything else illegible, overexposed. Even the laughing men still hide their slogans. Something prevails, the fat one in the shortsleeved shirt could be spelling out.

different banners. Plain cardboard tacked to roofing slats. In the borders of 800. He recognises himself on the photo: the laugh, the strong teeth, the non-iron nylon shirt with the only tie he possessed, the cheap health service glasses.

sorgfältig ein spruchband versöhnung. Im hintergrund die universität. Das geographische institut, der neubau der psychologen. Mit dem ort kehren zeit und ereignis zurück. Bonn im mai oder juni 1966, großdemonstration der vertriebenenverbände. Wenn sie von heimat reden, meinen sie großdeutschland und wenn sie selbstbestimmungsrecht sagen, wollen sie grenzrevisionen. Sie sind aus der ganzen bundesrepublik mit bussen angereist. 100 000 teilnehmer. Und unter ihnen er mit sechs genossen. SDS sozialistischer deutscher studentenverband und shb sozialdemokratischer hochschulbund. Sie tauchten ein, schwammen mit im strom der schlesier, pommern, sudetendeutschen, ostpreußen, donauschwaben, siebenbürgersachsen, baltendeutschen. Studenten in weißem hemd, mit schlips und adrettem haarschnitt. Sie wurden freundlich begrüßt. Man zeigte auf ihre transparente. Karl der große: deutschland in den grenzen von 800. Rache für den verlorenen krieg. Auch togo bleibt deutsch. Man spendete lob, daß sie den kampf der alten

Behind him on the right, his friend bernd r. Lost war, he can read. Then only fragments. A capital m, the final syllable itz. All made in the same way. Beside them, others are carefully fastening a banner reading: reconciliation. In the background, the university. The geographical institute and the new psychology building. With the place, memories of the time and circumstances return. Bonn, in may or june 1966: a major demonstration by the associations of expellees from the east. When they speak of a homeland, they mean greater germany, and when they talk of the right to self-determination they mean redrawing borders. They have come in buses from all over west germany. 100,000 of them. And among them, he himself and six comrades from the association of socialist german students and the social democratic university league. They dived in and swam with the tide of silesians, pomeranians, sudeten germans, east prussians, danube swabians, transylvanian saxons and baltic germans. Students in white shirts, with ties and smart

unterstützten. Gegen das unrecht von potsdam. Gegen die verbrecherischen prager beneschdekrete. Gegen die bonner verzichtpolitiker. Gegen die denkschrift der evangelischen kirche von deutschland, die frieden und versöhnung predigte. Gegen die botschaft der katholischen bischöfe polens, die vergebung heuchelte und anerkennung der grenzen wollte. Das unrecht wird nicht triumphieren. Stärker ist das heimatrecht.

manchmal blieben sie stehen mit ihren dachlatten und ließen den zug an sich vorbeiziehen. Pressefotografen stürzten sich auf sie. Knipsten immer wieder: auch togo bleibt deutsch. Als es mehr wurden, wuchs pötzlich das mißtrauen der marschierer. Stimmen. Finger zeigten auf sie. Der kleine gemütliche taucht wieder auf, dahinter der umriß des schlägers. Weißhaarige männer stürzten sich auf sie. Frauen mit perlenketten schrien. Herren mit schlips geiferten. Kommunistenschweine. Geht doch nach drüben. Vergasen sollte

haircuts. They received a friendly welcome. People pointed to their banners: charlemagne: germany in the borders of 800. Revenge for the lost war. Give togo back to the germans. They were congratulated on supporting the cause of the older generation. Against the injustice of the potsdam conference. Against the criminal benes decrees of prague. Aginst the politicians in bonn who wanted to waive their rights to land. Against the memorandum from the lutheran church in germany which preached peace and reconciliation. Against the message from the catholic bishops of poland which feigned forgiveness and wanted the borders recognised. Injustice shall not prevail. The right to a homeland is stronger.

from time to time they stood still with their roof slat banners and let the concourse move on past them. Press photographers swarmed towards them, clicking their cameras again and again: give togo back to the germans.

man euch. Sie schienen zu wissen, wovon sie sprachen. Grapschten nach den transparenten. Bildeten ketten. Versuchten einzukesseln. Fehlte gerade noch, daß sie sich an koppel und sturmriemen faßten.

mir fallen beim betrachten der gesichter auf den fotos nietzsches bemerkungen aus der «genealogie der moral» ein. Das ressentiment als haltung derjenigen, denen die tat versagt und nur eine imaginäre rache geblieben ist. Aber die hier hatten doch gelebt in einer zeit, als gehandelt wurde, hatten mitgehandelt. Nicht nur imaginär rache genommen, sondern reale blutströme fließen lassen quer durch europa. Nietzsche erklärt das ressentiment als nein zur außenwelt, als nein zum anderssein, als nein zu sich selbst. Nicht lebensbejahung aus sich heraus, sondern reaktion auf eine als feindlich begriffene welt. Das war die krankenakte der deutschen. Unsicher in ihrem nationalgefühl, wegen der jahrhundertelangen ohnmacht des reiches, traumatisiert durch die permanente innere zwietracht der deutschen

As more and more of them turned up, the marchers suddenly became suspicious. Voices. Fingers pointed at them. The short congenial chap reappears, and behind him the silhouette of the thug. White haired men lunged at them. Women in pearls screamed. Gentlemen in ties foamed with rage: «communist swine!», «go back to east berlin!», you're fit for the gas chambers!». They seemed to know what they were talking about. They grabbed at the banners, formed chains and tried to encircle the demonstrators. All they needed now was to grasp onto their belts and chest straps.

looking at the faces on the photographs, i am reminded of nietzsche's remarks in «on the genealogy of morals». Resentment as the attitude of those to whom action is denied and only an imaginary revenge remains. But the people here had, surely, lived in a time of action, and had joined in that action. Not only taking imaginary revenge, but causing real rivers of blood to flow right across europe.

stämme und ihrer führer, hatten sie einen neuen kaiser herbeigesehnt und ein neues reich, hatten ein einiges volks geträumt und eine heilige harmonie. Als die kluft zwischen ideal und wirklichkeit durch die niederlage von 1918 zu groß geworden war, hatten sie sich einen führer gerufen, der deutschland stark machte und eine volksgemeinschaft geschaffen, die all das endgültig ausschloß und ausmerzte, was ihnen fremd und feindlich erschien. Das ressentiment hatte sich vorübergehend und mit furchtbaren folgen als tat maskiert. Jetzt, 1966, war es wieder in der gewohnten rolle zu besichtigen. Der breitschultrige, der demagoge, der gemütliche, die nike, die beiden alten, der greis: alles opfer einer feindlichen welt, alle gepeinigt von dem wunsch nach imaginärer rache. Wir hatten dieser phantasie der rache ein gesicht gegeben auf unseren plakaten, hatten ihr orte und namen geliehen. Deshalb waren wir ihnen so vertraut gewesen und, als sie ihre bloßstellung erkannt hatten, so verhaßt geworden.

Nietzsche explains resentment as a no to the outside world, a no to being different, and as a no to oneself. Not an affirmation of life springing from the self, but a reaction to a world conceived of as hostile. That was the german disease. Uncertain in their national identity following the centuries of impotent empire, traumatised by the permanent inner discord between the german tribes and their leaders, they had summoned up a new emperor and a new empire, and dreamed of a united nation and a holy harmony. When the gap between the ideal and the reality became too great with the defeat of 1918, they had called for a führer to make germany strong and create a people's community which finally excluded and eliminated everything they found alien and hostile. Resentment had, temporarily and with frightful consequences, masqueraded as action. Now, in 1966, it could once again be observed in its accustomed role. The broad-shouldered thug, the demagogue, the congenial one, the nike, the two old women, the old man: all

 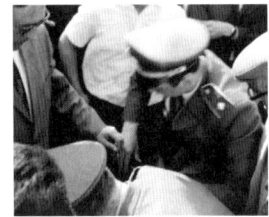 

die polizei interessierte sich plötzlich für uns. Wollte die plakate beschlagnahmen. Das große m: metz, toul und verdun. Die drei bistümer, die der kurfürst von sachsen 1552 aus dem reichsbesitz an den französischen könig heinrich II. verschachert hatte. Gerangel. Metz, toul und verdun fällt. Wird zerrissen, zertreten. Lutz k. hatte die pappe mit der aufschrift auschwitz getragen. Wie die vertriebenen ihre schilder breslau, memel, reichenberg und hermannstadt trugen. Die vertriebenen und heimatlosen von auschwitz. Geben sie das plakat her. Nein, was haben sie gegen auschwitz. Nichts, aber sie beteiligen sich an einer unangemeldeten demonstration. Vielleicht waren der polizeikommissar und seine helfer, die 1966 das recht gegen ein plakat durchsetzen wollten, 1941 via auschwitz zum osteinsatz gefahren, nach jozefow und lomazy, nach bialystok und riga, nach minsk und mogilew, zu all den kleinen auschwitz, die sie mit ihren polizeibataillonen veranstaltet hatten. Woher sonst all die wut.

of them victims of a hostile world, all tormented by the desire for imaginary revenge. We had put a face to this fantasy of revenge on our posters, and had given it names and places. That was why they had been so at home with us, and, on discovering they had been exposed, had hated us so much.

the police were suddenly interested in us, and wanted to confiscate the banners. The capital m: metz, toul and verdun – the three bishoprics in the holy roman empire of german nations which the elector of saxony bartered away to the french king henri ii in 1552. A skirmish ensued, and metz, toul and verdun fell, to be torn apart and trampled to the ground. Lutz k. had carried the cardboard poster with the inscription auschwitz. Just as the expellees had carried their signs with breslau, memel, reichenberg and hermannstadt. The expellees and homeless of auschwitz. «Give me the poster!» «No. What have you got against

togo entging der beschlagnahmung. Gegen das plakat fiel der polizei nichts ein. Wir hatten uns auf die hohen fenstersimse der universität geflüchtet. Standen dort. Mittelalterliche stifterfiguren. Karl der große: deutschland in den grenzen von 800. Das plakat fiel. Togo wurde in zwei teile gerissen. Wir wurden weitervertrieben. In einen nebenhof. Zurückgedrängt von einem polizeikessel. Meine letzte erinnerung: ich habe mich in die krone eines baumes gerettet und halte den rest einer pappe. Togo. La brèche.

auschwitz?» «Nothing, but you're taking part in an unregistered demonstration.» Perhaps the police chief and his helpers who wanted to impose the law on a poster in 1966 had travelled via auschwitz to their service in the east in 1941, to jozefov and lomazy, to bialystok and riga, to minsk and mogilev, to all the little auschwitzes they had created with their police battalions. Why else should they have been so enraged?

togo escaped seizure. The police could think of nothing to object to on the poster. We had fled onto the high window sills of the university and stood there like the statues of mediaeval benefactors. Charlemagne: germany in the borders of 800. The poster fell. Togo was torn in half. We were expelled from our pedestals, into a side alley, forced back by a line of police. My final memory: i escaped into the top of a tree, holding the remains of a piece of cardboard. Togo. La brèche. The breach. The gap.

hannes heer stammt aus den rechtsrheinischen wäldern, verbrachte seine schulzeit in einem kloster der cisterzienser und studierte geschichte, latein und germanistik in bonn und freiburg. 1965 konvertierte er aus dem katholizismus und der farbentragenden studentenverbindung «kdstv tuisconia königsberg» zum marxismus und gründete die bonner gruppe des sozialistischen deutschen studentenbundes (sds). Die presse kürte ihn wegen seines revolutionären elans und einiger spektakulärer einfälle zum «rudi dutschke von bonn», die landesregierung von nordrhein-westfalen verweigerte ihm trotz dieser belege für engagement und phantasie 1968 den zutritt zum schuldienst. Was damals «ein schreiendes unrecht» war, bezeichnet hannes heer heute als «glücksfall»: er ging zum rundfunk, arbeitete als regisseur und dramaturg an den schauspielhäusern in hamburg und köln, machte zehn jahre dokumentarfilme für zdf und ard und wurde dann mitarbeiter am forschungsinstitut des hamburger milliardärs und mäzens jan philipp reemtsma. Sein rheinisches naturell verließ ihn dabei nie: eine radio-sendung über den beitrag des us-ökonomen und nobelpreisträgers milton friedmann zum putsch gegen allende führte zu einer anfrage der cdu im bundestag, ein film über den atombunker der bundesregierung wurde vom wdr fünf minuten vor der sendung abgesetzt und seine arbeit für das hamburger institut war eine ausstellung über die verbrechen der deutschen wehrmacht 1941 bis 1944, die fast 1 million zuschauer fand, zu wütenden protesten führte und 1999 wegen zweier falscher bildunterschriften zurückgezogen wurde. Hannes heer erhielt 1997 die carl-von-ossietzky-medaille der internationalen liga für menschenrechte. Er arbeitet zur zeit an einem buch mit dem titel «die deutsche wehrmacht und der holocaust.».

hannes heer comes from the forests on the eastern side of the rhine. He spent his school days in a monastery of the cistercians and studied history, latin and german philology in bonn and freiburg. In 1965 he converted from catholicism and the colorful fraternity «kdstv tuisconia königsberg» to marxism and founded the bonn group of the socialist german fraternity (sds). The press declared him to be the «rudi dutschke of bonn» due to his revolutionary élan and a few spectacular ideas, and in 1968 the government of northrhine westphalia denied him the right to be a teacher despite this proof of commitment and imagination. What was a «flagrant injustice» back then is described by hannes heer today as «good fortune». He turned to radio and worked as a director and dramaturgist at the theaters in hamburg and cologne, made documentary films for zdf and ard for ten years and then became a collaborator at the research institute of the hamburg billionaire and sponsor jan philipp reemtsma. His rhinelandian temperament never deserted him along the way: a radio program about the contribution of the us economist and nobel prize winner milton friedmann to the putsch against allende led to an inquiry of the cdu in the bundestag, a film about the federal government's nuclear bunker was canceled five minutes before it was supposed to have been aired by wdr, and his work for the hamburg institute, an exhibition about the crimes of the german wehrmacht from 1941 to 1944 that was seen by almost one million visitors, caused angry protests and was withdrawn in 1999 due to two incorrect picture captions. Hannes heer received the carl von ossietzky medal of the international league of human rights in 1997. He is currently working on a book with the title «the german wehrmacht and the holocaust».

die vorbereitungen *the preparations*

köln, 19. september 2001:

tokujin + reiko yoshioka,
martin rendel, rené spitz

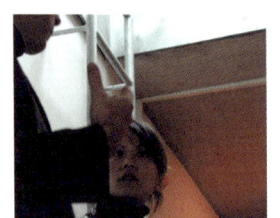

19.9.01

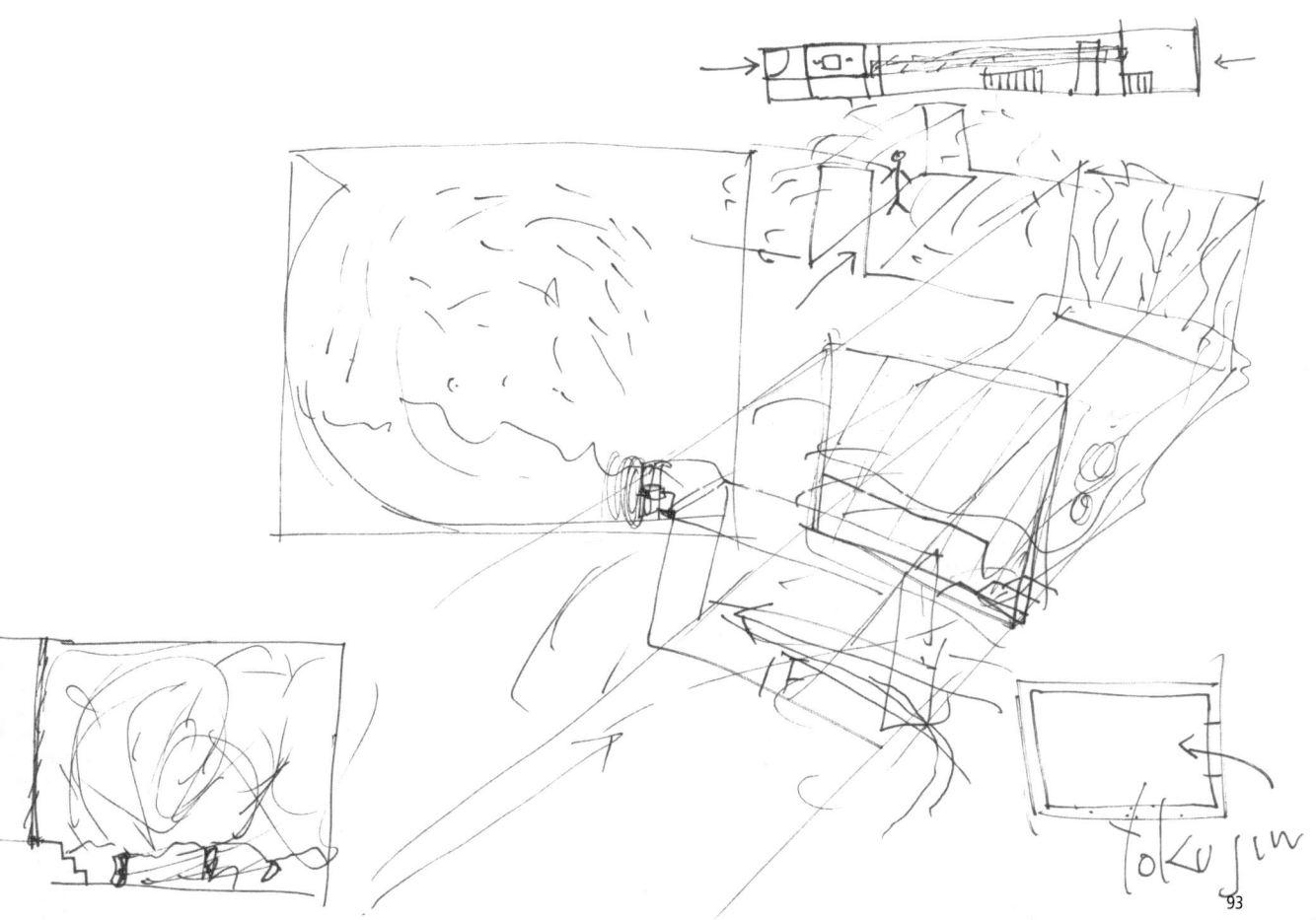

Tokujin

london, 23. september 2001:

greg lynn, ross lovegrove,
tokujin yoshioka;
mishka lovegrove;

reiko yoshioka;
greg lynn;

ross lovegrove

ross lovegrove entwirft
ross lovegrove designs

london, 23. september 2001

Lava lamps in colour which will arrive in a large box, hopefully simultaneously. until soon R.

special material

Dark space

Tokyo

solution A.
projection along upper ceiling surface.

Solution B
projection on lower ceiling surface only.

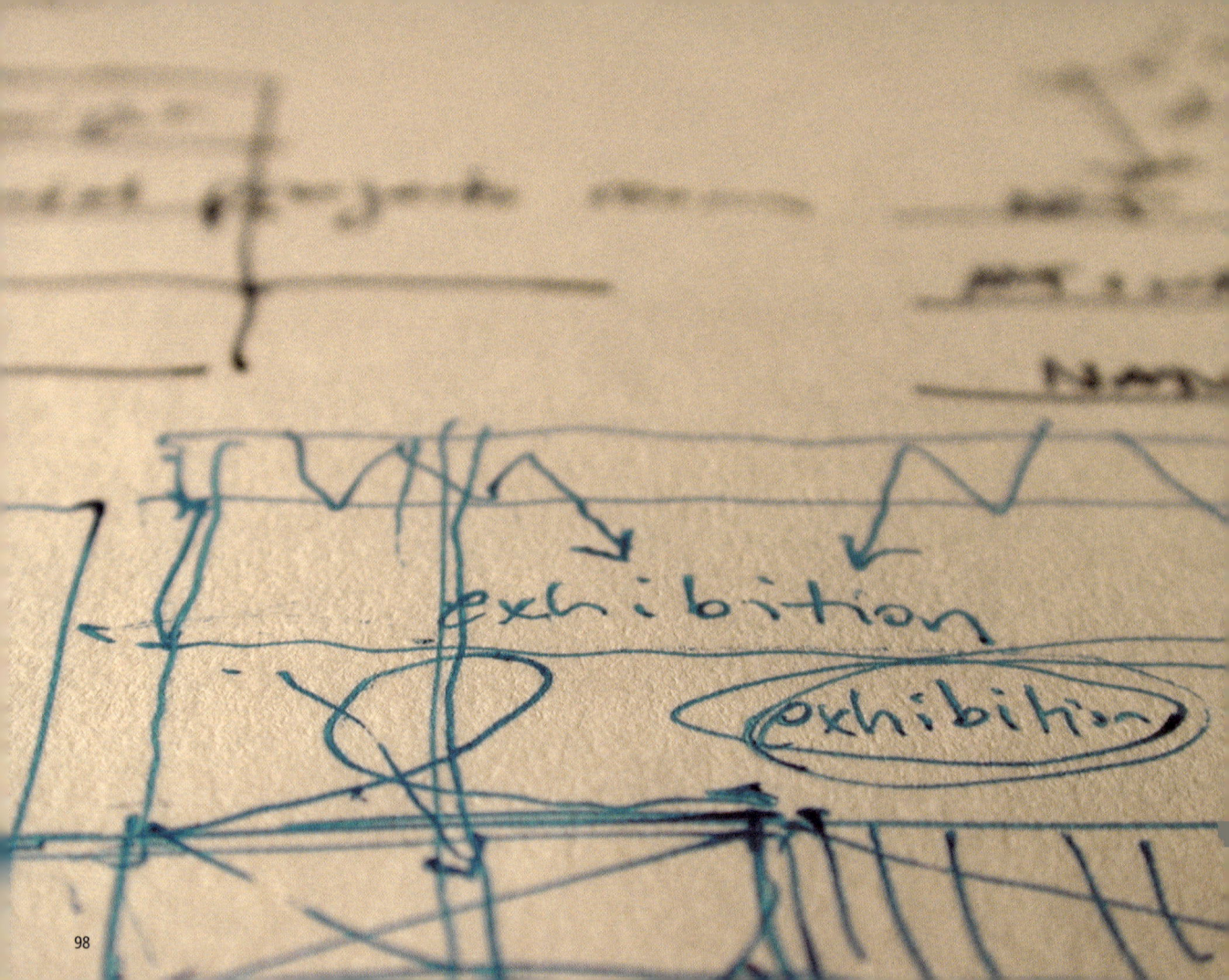

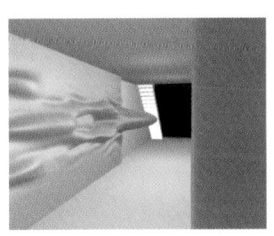 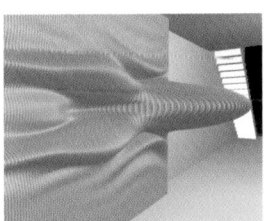 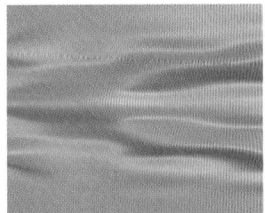 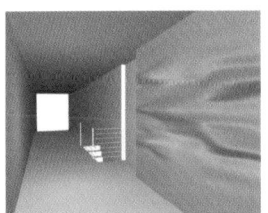

szenen aus einem animierten vor-entwurf greg lynns

scenes from an animated draft by greg lynn

das fräsen des entwurfs greg lynns
milling of the design by greg lynn

dezember 2001

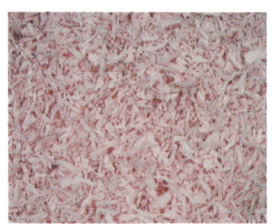 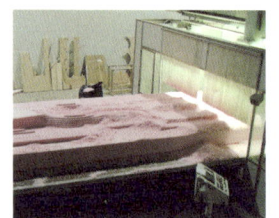

der fertige entwurf greg lynns
the finished design by greg lynn

19. dezember 2001

aufbau der installationen
assembly of the installations

15. dezember 2001

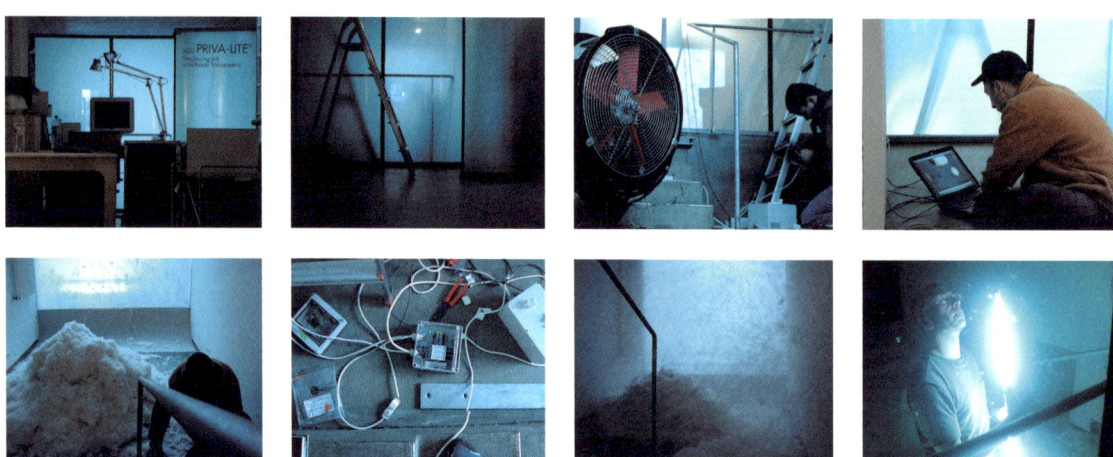

fotografie der installationen
photography of the installations

16. dezember 2001

  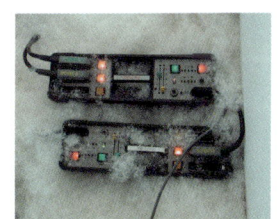 

das ergebnis *the result*

mit besonderem dank an
with special thanks to:

stefan beuttler
uli mattes
reiko yoshioka
jackilin hah
oliver bertram
marcelyn gow
franz schnaas
hannes heer
marion und dieter demski
thomas mayr-landsberg
anke bakker
marion zimmer
anke landsberg
hannah schaub
anja schröder
frank gössinger
david haberkamp
thomas kirschnick

sowie *as well as*:

austrotherm
cnc dynamix
liesegang
vegla
trimorph

bildnachweis *picture credit*

uli mattes, hamburg:
8, 18, 20-27, 44, 47-53, 106-112

lukas roth, köln:
14, 15

museum für gestaltung, zürich:
56-73

rendel & spitz, köln:
10, 11, 13, 30, 33-41, 92-98, 102-103

oliver bertram, eth zürich:
100

heinz engels, general-anzeiger, bonn:
76-77, 86-87

greg lynn form:
99, 101

unbekannt *unknown*:
78-89

franz schnaas, los angeles: 32
«068» from the series «proto type»
«0257» from «melancolic voltage»
«066» from «proto type»